Ministry of Education, Ontario
Information Services
13th Floor, Mowat Block, Queen's Park
Toronto   M7A 1L2

Assessment of Performance Unit

Communicating Mathematical Ideas

A practical interactive approach at ages 11 and 15

Lynn Joffe
Derek Foxman

London
Her Majesty's Stationery Office

© Crown 1989
First published 1989
ISBN 0 11 270656 8

Contents

	Page
Preface	v

		Page
1	**Introduction**	1
2	**The practical interactive setting**	3
	The efficacy of the practical interactive approach	3
	Attitudes and expectancies	4
	Mathematics in context: linking theory and practice	6
	Pupils using practical apparatus	10
	The challenge of activity-based tasks	13
	Getting started	16
	Summary and discussion points	17
3	**Communicating about mathematics**	19
	Talking	19
	Mathematical oracy	19
	Questioning	21
	Phrasing of questions	22
	Describing and explaining	23
	Being non-directive	26
	Prompting and probing	26
	Giving pupils time	29
	Recording	30
	Methods of recording	31
	Mathematical vocabulary	38
	Summary and discussion points	42
4	**Groups and group work**	43
	Introducing group work for the first time	43
	Setting up group situations	43
	Size and composition of groups	44
	Advantages and difficulties of group work	46

	Page
5 Assessment	48
Assessment of descriptions and explanations	48
Assessing groups and group work	51
Notes	55
Acknowledgements	57

Preface

The work discussed in this booklet was carried out by the Mathematics Research Team of the Assessment of Performance Unit (APU). The team was based at the National Foundation for Educational Research (NFER). The APU carries out surveys in the schools of England, Wales and Northern Ireland in several areas of the curriculum. The mathematics surveys are of 11-year-old pupils in primary or middle schools and 15-year-olds in secondary schools.

This booklet is principally concerned with aspects of the mathematics assessments which were administered in the surveys by experienced teachers, nominated by their LEAs, who were specially trained as assessors. These assessments have a practical and oral emphasis; the assessors can observe what pupils do and interact with them about the work. They contrast with written tests and attitude questionnaires which are also used in the surveys and are administered by the survey pupils' own teachers.

During the phase of annual surveys which started in 1978 and continued until 1982, the practical tests consisted of one-to-one interviews with survey pupils. The next surveys were carried out in 1987. In the intervening five years some further study was undertaken of the one-to-one interview situation and assessments of groups of three pupils undertaking a problem-solving task were developed; it is this further study and development work which provides the main material for this booklet.

The practical assessors were trained at a residential briefing using videotapes of the assessment situation, simulations and practice with pupils. Between the briefing and the survey they practised administering the assessments in their own schools.

The APU Language Team, also based at the NFER, contributed to the work recorded in this booklet.

1
Introduction

Increasing interest is being focused on how pupils communicate mathematical ideas and what factors facilitate or hinder their thinking and performance. This booklet features a selection of discussions and examples that illustrate aspects of how 11- and 15-year-olds demonstrate their mathematical knowledge in written, spoken and practical forms.

The bulk of the information was collected during the APU one-to-one practical mathematics surveys and the development work leading up to them, with some small school-based studies interjected. Additional work was carried out with classes of 11- and 15-year-olds working in groups of two, three or four pupils during 1985 and 1986.

Many of the features mentioned here form part of everyday classroom interaction, but perhaps have not been the focus of particular attention, partly because of time constraints and partly because they may have been thought insignificant. Also, many of the techniques discussed are used as a matter of course in other subjects, but may not be considered suitable or appropriate for mathematics by some teachers. Our finding [in the APU Mathematics Research Team] has been that these ideas are not particularly widespread in mathematics and many teachers, while interested, are not sure where to start.

Material for inclusion has been chosen in consultation with teachers and advisers in several local education authorities (LEAs). We are grateful to them for their help and co-operation. We hope that this booklet provides some starting-points for discussion and for classroom investigation, as well as for INSET (in-service teacher training) and staff development.

Your enquiries may lead you along different paths from those we have taken. We would be interested in hearing about these.

A number of examples of pupils' working on practical topics referred to in this booklet are taken from the APU videotapes. The videotapes were distributed in 1986 to LEAs and institutions concerned with initial teacher training in the APU practical kits containing material from the APU Mathematics, Language and Science surveys.

2

The practical interactive setting

The efficacy of the practical interactive approach

Some pupils can demonstrate their knowledge more effectively in a practical interactive setting than is evident from their more formal written work.[1] The opportunity to show physically what they can do and to talk about it gives them a wider range of possibilities. Such an opportunity was provided in the APU one-to-one practical situation, where pupils were asked to carry out tasks, usually involving apparatus.

In APU surveys, similar tasks that have appeared in both written and practical modes have a much lower non-response rate in the latter. There may be several reasons for this. First, the presentation is oral which removes the potential problems of pupils misreading, or being unable to read, the question. Secondly, the presentation is interactive so any misunderstanding of the question can be probed or prompted. Thirdly, pupils are under some pressure to respond because of the presence of an assessor.

A good example of a pupil responding well in a practical setting is Louise, a quiet 11-year-old. According to her teacher, she is unwilling to do any sort of written work or recording in mathematics and as a result spends most of her time in the remedial mathematics group. However, in a class exercise based on an APU Mass topic, she came up with an answer and explanation about finding the mass of one tile given several tiles, a balance and a 20-gram mass. She stuck to it despite criticism from a large proportion of the class, including the most dominant boys. She showed her findings to be correct using practical apparatus and went on to tackle further tasks in a confident manner which surprised her teacher. This incident also led the teacher to re-evaluate her expectations of Louise.

In other instances seemingly capable pupils have had difficulties relating their theoretical knowledge to the practical situation.

---

1 For notes see p. 55.

However, whether in practical work pupils rise above or fall below expectations based on their written work, teachers have reported that watching pupils use practical apparatus, both in straightforward tasks and for solving problems, sheds light on the methods they adopt and the strategies they use. The main focus is on the ways in which pupils reach their answers. For example, using a balance or other apparatus, pupils can show whether or not they understand what is meant by 'heavier' and 'lighter', or, in designing a package, it becomes clearer what notions they hold of shape, measurement and scale, especially if the observations are accompanied by interactive discussion on the pupils' work. This section gives illustrations of a number of factors which affect pupils' approaches.

Attitudes and expectancies

Pupils' experiences in and out of the classroom lead many of them to have certain attitudes and expectations about the ways in which they should tackle mathematical tasks, about the nature of mathematics and about the results that they can expect. A number of these have been highlighted in APU findings. Examples of expectations about tackling practical tasks are given below.

i) *Calculations should work out exactly*
A number of 11-year-old pupils working on one task in the Mass topic demonstrated an expectation that what they were asked to calculate would 'work out exactly' (no remainders). If this did not happen, they thought that they had made a mistake.

The task was to find the mass of one tile given a balance, a 20-gram mass and a bag of tiles, and pupils were most perturbed at finding that 21 tiles had a mass of 20-grams.

Some responses to this situation were:
    Assessor: What have you discovered?
    Shivani: There are 21 weights [tiles, that have a mass of 20 grams] so I think that might be a bit wrong...There's one extra.

Other pupils hid one tile or chose to ignore the fact that the pointer on the balance was not centred.

ii) *There is one correct solution*
There also seems to be a high expectation amongst pupils that there is only one correct solution to every problem. While this has

probably been their experience in most instances, many pupils, mainly 15-year-olds, feel that this should be the case whatever the situation. With more open problems, it takes some time before pupils accept that there may be a variety of appropriate responses.

iii) *Mathematics is arithmetic*
This response often appears in the APU attitude questionnaire, and has been observed in practical work. One 15-year-old girl happily carried out a number of tasks in the Mass topic using a balance (not always correctly) to compare blocks, weigh lumps of plasticine, etc. The final task was to find the mass of a small tile given several tiles and a 20-gram mass. She found that 35 tiles weighed 20-grams and, realising she had to do a calculation said, distastefully, 'Oh, maths. I'm no good at maths'.

iv) *Mathematics is not used in everyday situations*
Pupils who have worked on the 'everyday' problem-solving topics often reject the idea that they are doing any mathematics. 'This isn't maths, it's common sense' is a frequent statement, or 'It's just life'. The origins of the attitude may be in the pupils' out-of-school experiences and in primary schools where much teaching of mathematics is carried out in the context of everyday activities such as shopping. These activities are not clearly defined as mathematics whereas 'doing sums' is.

Another aspect of the divide between school and everyday experiences is the differing use of terminology and measurement units in the two contexts. Many pupils in secondary schools have been brought up to use the metric system exclusively in school, whereas the outside world frequently uses imperial units. If asked how tall they are they will give their height in feet and inches, whereas distances assumed to be in a mathematical or scientific context are more likely to be given in metric system units.

The correct scientific usage of terms such as 'weight' and 'mass' is problematic for many pupils: written test items in mathematics have a higher success rate if the everyday term is used. In the practical topics pupils are given the option of referring to a mass as such or as a 'weight'. The majority prefer the everyday term.

If mathematics is to be appreciated in a range of contexts, as the Cockcroft Committee recommended[10], it is important for pupils to have an awareness of the distinctive register of terms used in each context. They also need to be able to deal adequately with the measurement units employed. Personal measures such as height and weight may be good starting-points for comparing imperial and metric units and for distinguishing between the different scientific meanings of terms such as 'weight' and 'mass'.

v) *Using calculators is cheating*
This view has been encountered with both 11- and 15-year-olds in the practical surveys. A few assessors in the surveys of older pupils commented that, when calculators were provided as an aid in solving problems, some pupils were reluctant to use them. They saw using them as cheating, or thought they would get less credit if they were used instead of doing their calculations with pencil and paper.

Such pupils need experience of judging what means of calculation is most appropriate in a particular situation—mental, pencil and paper or electronic calculator—and knowing that credit is given for a justified choice.

Mathematics in context: linking theory and practice

We have commented that many pupils do not regard everyday situations as providing opportunities to do some mathematics. Nevertheless some mathematics, especially calculation, is carried out in everyday situations. How does pupils' social knowledge interact with their mathematical performance? One topic which highlights this aspect is that of deciding which offer of a particular item is a 'best buy'. The largest quantity packaged is usually expected to provide the best value (assuming that the customer can make use of all the contents of a large package), but there are instances when this is not so. Many pupils, when asked which of two sizes of washing-up liquid and of three sizes of coffee are the best buys, give answers like:

> 'I'd say the big one.'
> 'My Mum would buy the big one.'

In an example in a practical topic, over 20 per cent of both age groups have had to be prompted to calculate the actual differences in price. However, the price relationships were complex in these examples. In another 'best buy' example a number of pupils who chose the more expensive option gave a reasonable argument for their choice. This occurred in the topic for 11-year-olds, 'Organising a Birthday Party'. The pupils were given the option of buying six packets of crisps at 10p per small packet or a family pack at 45p (containing, they are told, the same amount as six small packets).

Nearly 20 per cent of the sample chose the more expensive alternative.

Their reasons for this choice were varied:

> 'Although it costs more, if you have six separate packets there will be no fighting over who has the most.'
> 'Not everyone likes the same flavour; if you get small packets you can have different flavours.'

When asking pupils why they opted for one size rather than the other, it became clear that many had been aware that in pure economic terms the family pack was better value for money. However, in their view, 'value for money' was not purely related to the arithmetic, it had a broader social connotation. As illustrated in the comments above, it was not seen as cost effective or good value to buy a family pack, if it was going to lead to squabbling or dissatisfaction. Similarly, when the term 'best buy' is used, the assessment of what is best often includes some social considerations.

There are situations in which there is a mismatch between theoretically known 'truths' and what happens in reality and pupils find it difficult to account for this. They often know that in theory a particular event should occur but are not able to give an explanation if it does not occur in practice.

An example of this concerns a topic on 'probability': many 11- and 15-year-olds were able to give the theoretical probability of a coin landing on heads or tails or a die showing a given number when thrown. When they were asked to carry out a small-scale exercise related to this, they were often confused by the fact that their data did not match those predicted. This often led to a loss of confidence in their predictions or they resorted to idiosyncratic explanations like:

> 'When my dad tosses a coin, it always lands on heads.'
> 'I must have been throwing the dice wrong.'
> 'When I'm playing at home, I always get a 6.'

Both 11- and 15-year-olds often insist that the number of heads or tails (using coins) or sixes (using dice) that come up will depend on *how* you throw the coin or the dice. In the 'real' context of the topic, this can in fact have an influence; however, this may be obscuring the aim, which is to examine the idea of probability as an abstraction or idealisation of actual processes. This point is not exclusive to the practical situation but is one which comes up often in this context.

An important point appears to be that more emphasis needs to be placed on the relationship between theory and practice. Pupils do not seem comfortable with questioning either the theory or what happens in practice and so will often accept different answers to the same problem obtained by different methods.

In a topic in the first APU primary survey pupils were asked to do a verbal problem printed on a sheet of paper (eg 'Brian has 64p in his pocket. He buys a scrapbook for 28p. How much money has he left?'). Some pupils used the pencil and paper that was available and others obtained the answer mentally. The latter pupils were then presented with the equivalent calculation out of context (eg 64−28) and asked to do it as they would in class. Most pupils worked out the verbal problems in their heads, usually by complementary addition, whereas, on paper, most used standard procedures or algorithms they had been taught in their classrooms.

Assessors' comments included a number such as 'Pupil did not seem to relate the different answers achieved'; 'Pupil treated problem and algorithm as two separate entities'; 'Pupil did not recognise the problem and the algorithm as the same'.

This raises the whole question of the relationship between formal and informal knowledge and the links pupils make (or not, as the case may be) between things they have learnt. There seem to be occasions when mention of a particular term, or the provision of a piece of apparatus, acts as a trigger for the use of certain procedures or formulae. For example, questions about the area of a shape are often the cue for the formula for finding the area of a rectangle, 'length times breadth'. However, if one asks about covering a floor or using a grid, more 'informal', less standard ideas are often put forward.

Another example of the theory/practice split is that of a child who tried to find the mass of one plastic tile having found that 21 tiles have a mass of 20 grams. The oral answer was that each tile had a mass greater than one gram; however, as soon as she was offered pencil and paper, a written set of procedures appeared to be evoked and she calculated the correct answer. She was unable to reconcile successfully the practically-based and the rule-based solutions—she gave an incorrect oral answer and continued to justify it, despite contradictory written evidence.

In the Area topic (age 11), some pupils appear to fixate on one form of measurement (eg ruler or square centimetre grid) and appear not to associate the formula (the area of a rectangle as its length times breadth) with measuring, using a grid.

Pupils may also have difficulty in relating number patterns to a concrete representation. In the Number Rods topic, 11-year-olds are asked to predict, then find out, how many ways there are of making given lengths, using different Cuisenaire rods. Pupils who do not find all the permutations, or who include repetitions, are corrected. When they predict the number of permutations a 'my guess' card is placed above the rods showing their guess. Once they have found all the permutations successively for each length of rod the 'my guess' card is replaced by a card bearing the correct number. The 'my guess' cards are left in view displayed above the correct number cards (see diagram below).

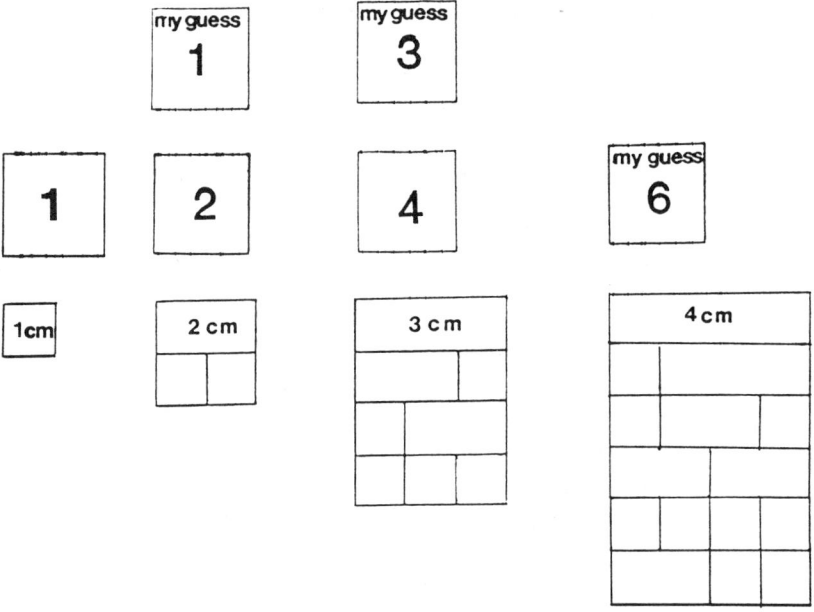

Even though pupils have cards with the correct number of permutations in front of them, and they have made each permutation, they still find it difficult to divorce the emerging number sequence from the rods themselves. Some pupils, when asked to guess the next number of permutations in the sequence (eg 'How many arrangements of rods can be made which are 4 cm long?'), stare for some time at the last set of permutations before giving their answer. When asked how they got their estimate their answers indicate that they were attempting to construct the arrangement mentally. This is not an easy thing to do, but having done it, it is not difficult to confirm the estimate by making just that number of arrangements given in the estimate. Other pupils chose to extend the number sequence in accordance with the pattern they identified. Fewer pupils correctly extended the number sequence in this topic compared with a written test question asking for the next two terms in the sequence 1−2−4−8. Although assessors referred pupils who took the practical topic to the number sequence as well as the rods, it seems likely that the reason for the lower success rate was due to pupils' attention being taken up by the rods and their arrangements and with ensuring their predictions were fulfilled.

Pupils using practical apparatus

Pupils' familiarity (or lack of it) with practical apparatus may be inferred from the ways in which they use the apparatus.

Sometimes the evidence is direct. For example, in 1982, in a topic in which a calculator was used, 20 per cent of the 11-year-olds asked said that they had not used a calculator before. Most of this group were able to carry out simple calculations with one but did not know how to clear the display.

Also in 1982, only 10 per cent of 11-year-old pupils said that they used a calculator in class; comments like 'We're not allowed that sort of thing' were frequent. Nearly 70 per cent said that they used a calculator at home. Of course, this situation may have changed by now, though evidence collected during trials in 1986 suggests that this was still the case in some schools at that time.

Some 15-year-old pupils may show reluctance to use a calculator when one is provided but its use is optional. We have already noted that some pupils seem to hold the view that using a calculator is cheating. Others prefer to use a familiar pencil-and-paper procedure in situations where a calculator could otherwise provide a more rapid answer.

Pupils' use of seemingly familiar apparatus such as a ruler can yield surprises. For example, in a Length topic (age 11), 8 per cent of pupils did not use a ruler properly to measure a straight line and had to be taught. The most common problem amongst these pupils was that they did not align the beginning of the scale with the line to be measured; they aligned the end of the ruler, with the beginning of the line irrespective of where the scale began. This use of a ruler has been noted also in the group problem-solving tasks.

When measuring the adjacent side of a rectangular shape some pupils are observed to keep the ruler in a horizontal position and turn the shape after measuring the first side. Others keep the shape in the same position and rotate the ruler to a vertical position. Another strategy observed in the measurement of the sides of a square is to place the ruler parallel to a side instead of along it. These methods may not all be sufficiently adequate if very accurate measurements are required.

Familiarity with measurement situations is as important as familiarity and practice with measuring devices. For example, a group of fourth-year secondary pupils used a steel tape to measure one another's heights. They did not all ensure that the person being measured was upright, or that the tape was vertical. Some 11-year-olds, working in groups of three pupils, were given a similar task and a large proportion of them failed to do so accurately. They were far more adept at measuring the lengths of rectangular objects such as tables.

During a survey, an APU assessor reported that one pupil chose a tape measure to find the circumference of a cylindrical tin. The tape was wrapped carefully round the tin and then, before the assessor realised what was happening, the pupil took a pair of scissors and snipped off the tape which was in excess of the circumference!

On another occasion, a tape measure was chosen to measure a wavy line. Other apparatus available was a ruler and some string. Here, the pupil recognised that a ruler was inappropriate because something flexible was needed to follow the contour of the line. The need to measure with a properly graduated scale overtook consideration of other possible strategies.

Sometimes, though, the reasons for choice of apparatus are more idiosyncratic. When asked why he used different apparatus for apparently similar tasks, one boy replied: 'I just like using different things.' This may also have been because he felt that he had to use all the apparatus that was supplied. It is often the case that, when pupils are set a task by a teacher, they expect that everything provided has a role to play in finding an answer.

However, it is also a common observation that many pupils need permission to use apparatus. For example, after weighing out a 20 gram lump of plasticine using a balance and a 20 gram mass, the 20 gram mass was removed and pupils were asked to make a lump half as heavy (11-year-olds) or a quarter as heavy (15-year-olds).

Although the balance was still immediately in front of them a number of pupils did not use it for the task. Instead they either estimated the division of the lump of plasticine by eye or were unsure how to start. Sometimes, indicating the balance, a tentative 'Should I use this?' emerged.

The difference between seeking permission to use apparatus and situations in which pupils feel they have to use what is provided would seem to lie in their familiarity with the apparatus and its range of use; a ruler is commonly used in the classroom and so, if provided, should be used. A balance is rather more rarely used and the task of dividing a lump of plasticine could be carried out by other means. However, several pupils who initially did not use the balance for this task showed later that they knew it could be used; they simply needed reassurance that it was permissible to do so.

Finally in this section we note a very curious phenomenon which we have called 'the one-arm syndrome': there are a number of pupils who are apparently reluctant to use both hands for a task, even when it would make the task easier for them. An example of this may be seen on the APU videotape (Age 11) (see Introduction p. 1) on the Mass topic where Shivani first finds which of two rectangular blocks is the heavier and then places these two, and then a third block, in order of mass. She uses only one hand for these tasks and brings the other into play only when she is forced to: to manipulate a piece of plasticine in order to weigh out 20 grams of it. Some observers have suggested that it is an indication of unease in the situation, whilst others suggest that it may be a lack of familiarity with the apparatus or a cultural feature.

There is a more general point here, though; the way pupils use apparatus may give some clues to their understanding of, and attitude towards, mathematics.

The challenge of activity-based tasks

Practical mathematics does not consist simply of weighing and measuring. These are procedures which may be used in the course of working on larger-scale problems. Although some topics in the one-to-one APU practical surveys have been concerned with specific skills or concepts, there are also larger-scale 'everyday' and investigatory topics such as planning a day out or investigating arrangements of tiles. Extracts from interviews with pupils on these topics can be seen on the APU Age 11 (Class Trip) and Age 15 (Tiles) videotapes. Whole problems were also used for the APU surveys of group problem-solving. Some features of the development work for these surveys form the subject of a later section of this booklet. The APU booklet *Practical Mathematics—Assessing Practical Mathematics in Secondary Schools*[2] proposed four meanings which could be given to the term 'practical' in 'practical mathematics':

i) 'Empirical'—concerned with knowledge gained through observation and experimentation. Scientific and other empirical investigations can provide mathematical data and mathematical patterns.

ii) 'Construction'—using materials and apparatus to make things which require the use of mathematical skills such as measuring and knowledge of spatial relationships.

iii) Concrete modelling of mathematical concepts and relationships.

iv) Practical situations such as those in everyday life which involve mathematical skills.

Perhaps games and puzzles should be added as a fifth category.

Not all of the practical interactive topics have a specifically practical element in the narrow sense of using materials or apparatus which are manipulable. There is no clear-cut division between practical and non-practical; each of the above categories of 'practical' has associated non-practical aspects: for example, experiments and practical everyday situations in the classroom have to be planned, and constructions designed. Practical work has to be thought out as well as carried out, and evaluated as well as completed.

It is not difficult to identify features of mathematical tasks which may put pupils off. In the APU mathematics attitude questionnaire pupils were asked to comment on some written test items. Here are comments made about two items:

A car's speed, v, is given by the formula $v = u + at$
where u is the initial speed
    a is the constant acceleration
    t is the time taken.

Calculate the speed of a car which starts from rest
and accelerates at 0.5 m/s^2 for 15 seconds.   ....m/s

A car starts with a speed of 11 m/s and accelerates at
0.8 m/s^2. How long will it take to reach a speed of
15 m/s?   ....s

'Too many words to describe this question makes it seem difficult.'

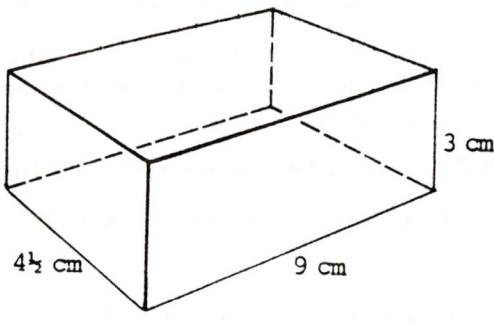

What is the volume of this rectangular block?

.......cm^3

'We have not learnt about volumes, but just looking at the question makes me feel I don't want to know about them.'

It is not specifically written test material which is at fault, since thematic tests—those built round situations rather than around particular concepts and skills—have received very favourable responses from pupils. Many pupils also find interesting the Problems and Patterns written tests which were introduced into APU mathematics surveys in 1981. However, practical situations with manipulable materials or interactive topics do appear to be particularly involving. But is the pupil's involvement with the task or with the apparatus?

When asked to estimate different lengths, many pupils used their finger width, pencil width and various other idiosyncratic methods to assist them. Sometimes, though, these methods replaced the task in hand. For example, when converting a length into a distance, using a scale, some pupils became so involved in measuring in finger widths they forgot that they were supposed to estimate the distance between a and b. It may be that these techniques need to be encouraged, but perhaps tempered with considerations of the rationale behind their uses.

In the Number Rods task some pupils found the manipulation of the rods so involving that the original task began to slip away. Of course, getting bogged down in procedures and so losing sight of the task is a complaint which could be and has been made about complex arithmetic in naturalistic problem-solving in the days before calculators became generally available. The important factor is that the procedures necessary to solve a problem, whether practical or otherwise, should be within a pupil's competence and sufficiently familiar to enable the pupil to keep the task in view.

Some practical tasks that had immediate appeal, and during which persistence and enjoyment were evident, were those that pupils did not see as mathematical—such as planning a day out or an exhibition, or catering for a birthday party. Pupils worked individually and in groups for up to two hours on such tasks, without showing signs of boredom. Low-attaining fourth-year pupils, described as 'difficult' by their teacher, were also observed to work intently for over an hour when introduced to a 'circus' of short practical tasks[3]. More purely mathematical topics, without apparatus, can also engage pupils' attention for a considerable period if the problem is found to be challenging. That is, they have an opportunity to try out their own ideas and develop their own methods. Such problems have been used by the APU in both one-to-one and group situations.

Teachers may be cautious about introducing to older pupils apparatus which looks like younger children's play equipment. When developing one topic for 15-year-olds which involved the use of a set of 2-centimetre wooden cubes, a pupil was asked whether she thought such apparatus was 'babyish'. She replied, 'Not if the problem is challenging.' Thus the essential feature of activity-based learning might well be the challenge of the task, not necessarily the use of apparatus, although materials can be attracting.

Getting started

Getting started with practical and investigative work generally is not easy, but a number of teachers had successfully introduced it before the GCSE national criteria incorporated it as a requirement to be implemented by 1991.

The growing literature on practical and investigative mathematics in the classroom is still mostly to be found in journals such as *Mathematics Teaching* and *Mathematics in School*. There are some ideas about classroom organisation for practical work in the APU booklet *Practical Mathematics—Assessing Practical Mathematics in Secondary Schools*[4] and some information in introducing group work is included in a later section of this booklet.

Here is a teacher from one of the teachers' groups who assisted with this booklet describing how he started off an investigation:

> One of my favourite starting-points is:
> Form a chain of numbers using the rule 'Multiply the units digit by 2, add to the tens digit and repeat'. We start with an example, say 37, and ask for the next term which we discuss as there are often differing interpretations of the rule.
>
> I then encourage the pupils to provide the next few terms as a group and ask them to describe any patterns that appear to be starting as a result of each new term. We then note whether these patterns continue. After a few terms I then ask them to continue the chain, and silence generally descends for a few minutes. Whilst some race on, producing one number after another without attempting to notice anything, others seek patterns more slowly and others need help with the next term, having not really understood a word so far! As things happen in the chain the discussion begins. Some pupils 'finish', having 'sussed it', and need encouragement to look again and see what else they notice or to try it again with a different starting number. Some pupils are inquisitive enough to try things for themselves; one pupil, having noticed the repeating chain, thought this was a good way to complete two whole pages of work and kept writing the chain down over and over again.
>
> The teacher does not need to tell the pupils anything. If the pupil asks a question the reply can be a question: 'Do you think all numbers do the same? If not, which ones don't? Or, can you prove that all numbers obey your rule? Are those that

work, or those that do not, connected? What happens if you change the rule and multiply by 3, 4, 5...?'

The last question, 'What happens if...', is really the key to working in an investigative way. It is the question that the teacher really wants the pupils to ask for themselves but it helps at the outset if the teacher keeps asking it. Sometimes the teacher will know the answer and sometimes not. In previous situations teachers were expected to know the answer and frequently only set the questions they knew they could do. In these activities it gives the pupils considerable satisfaction to know that they have discovered something not known by their teacher. It also frequently keeps the teacher interested in the activity. Many teachers have commented that they have had their interest in mathematics re-awakened by setting these activities.

By introducing activities initially within the current organisation, the pupils are less likely to regard them with the same suspicion that they would if the classroom were re-organised at the outset. Group work can be developed naturally. In the Number Chain example, one way to prove whether the same chain works for all two digit numbers is to try it on all two digit numbers. This work could be shared between a group of pupils. Some activities require some apparatus, cubes for example. Frequently classrooms are not equipped for each pupil to have sufficient of these and group work is the natural solution to the problem. Group work can therefore be introduced gradually.

Summary and discussion points

In this section we have considered some points to look out for when introducing and observing practical and investigative activities. The main points can be summarised as follows:

i) Practical work in mathematics should be seen in the context of wider-scale experimentation, construction, modelling and everyday planning activities.

ii) Practical work focuses on processes which may reveal more of a pupil's thought and ideas than products do. The APU practical interviews have revealed that some pupils have limited perceptions about the nature of mathematics. Their expectations about the task, what they can use to undertake it, and the sort of answer that might be appropriate can all influence their responses in particular situations. More experience of mathematics in context and appreciation of the appropriate use of resources such as calculators may change these perceptions.

iii) Practical work tends to be involving, but the involvement can be with the manipulation of the apparatus rather than with the task. However, practical work in mathematics is not to be regarded as a soft option. Planning and reviewing experiments and designing and evaluating constructions can be thought-provoking activities.

3

Communicating about mathematics

Talking

Mathematical oracy

> 'It is only recently that pupils' spoken language skills have come into prominence as an area of interest to teachers and educationalists.'[5]

This is the view of the APU Language Team when referring to oracy in the classroom generally. It is even more recently that this interest in spoken language has turned towards talk in relation to mathematics.

The Language Team go on to say that a relatively small proportion of teaching time and expertise has been devoted to developing pupils' speaking and listening skills. An informal survey of mathematics classrooms visited during the course of the development of APU materials revealed that almost no work of this type was being done intentionally.

It is more common to find pupils working alone on individualised schemes or within a fairly formal teacher-directed 'chalk-and-talk' session. Although pupils may be invited to discuss in such lessons, researchers like Flanders (1970)[6] and Shuard (1985)[7] have found that the quality and quantity of talk is typically limited—'both in terms of the amount of talk allocated to each pupil, and in terms of pupils' relegation to the role of passive respondents to teacher-initiatives'. Dale Spender (1981)[8] has also illustrated that mathematics teachers may respond differently to boys and girls and ask them qualitatively different questions.

An integral part of APU practical testing has been the talk about mathematics that is generated, both formally through scripted questions and probes, and informally when pupils volunteer information or chat generally. From this and other interviews, it seems that many pupils, particularly at secondary level, do not consider that mathematics is something that is open to discussion and negotiation. Many of the techniques used in APU settings (and those of other projects) for eliciting knowledge and information have provoked much interest amongst teacher groups. Some of these are discussed below.

The value of asking pupils about mathematical thinking should not be underestimated; insights can be gained into how pupils have interpreted (ie 'learnt') information that has been 'taught'. At a very basic level, asking pupils to say numbers may give teachers a clue as to their understanding. Take the decimal 0.35 for example; the pupil who reads that as 'zero point thirty-five' may be thinking of numbers on either side of the decimal point as similar and perhaps does not understand the relationships within the number system[9].

A more extreme example was collected during an interview with Jason, an 11-year-old, as part of a study to encourage pupils to talk about APU written test items. Jason's ordering of one-place decimals (0.3, 0.1, 0.7, 0.6) seemed sound, but as more complex examples were discussed it became apparent that something was amiss. Finally, the 'problem' for the teacher, not Jason) came to light as follows:

> Jason (reading the question out loud to the assessor):
> 'Put these decimals in order of size, smallest first: 0.064, 0.35, 0.64, 1.1. (says numbers) Zero point zero six four, zero point three five, zero point six four, one point one.'

> 'This looks a bit tricky at first... it looks a catch but it's not really, I don't think, because 1.1 will go first because it's got a one at the start instead of a zero; so that will go highest 'cause I'm working my way down.'

> 'Then the second... this is a bit tricky the second for me. I think they'd both share second, because it's got 0.64 and 0.064 and I don't think that that first zero after the point doesn't sort of matter... I think they'd share the same place... But there again that zero might mean zero a bit, sort of a bit down from the 0.64... as an answer they'd be joint second and then as a last one it would be 0.35 'cause that is lower than 0.64 and 1.1.'

If he had not been questioned about his working, it might have been assumed that he was confused as to biggest and smallest decimals—he was not, he just found it difficult to deal with the question in its given form.

Questioning

An important issue to emerge from the practical surveys and one that provokes much discussion at teachers' meetings is that of questioning. Assessors in the surveys have repeatedly expressed surprise and interest in how different ways of questioning lead to different responses from pupils. For example, the way in which questions are worded and where they are interjected can have a profound effect on whether pupils are able to respond and may influence the responses they give.

Most of the APU practical scripts are designed so that questions are graded by difficulty. Initial questions are straightforward; generally, their purpose is to familiarise pupils with the apparatus required and/or the situation around which the topic revolves. Also, the inclusion of easier questions ensures that lower attainers have the chance to answer at least some questions with confidence, which will hopefully give them a sense of achievement and encourage all pupils to attempt further questions.

As the interview progresses, harder questions test knowledge and some basic applications of the knowledge. The final questions are generally the most difficult; they are intended to test more complex applications, understanding or ability to solve problems and are necessary if one is to stretch the more able in the class. A valuable aspect of APU script construction is that if pupils are struggling, the topic can be abandoned without them being aware that the script has not been completed.

The way 'why?' and 'when?' questions are asked or interjected is important. To some extent the timing and nature of questions depends on the nature of the task during which questions are put, the types of question and the age of the pupils being questioned.

Pupils are told at the beginning of their interviews that they will be asked about how they obtained their answers and that this does not mean that the answers they have given are right or wrong: the assessor is interested in the methods they use. Some pupils still think that they must have made a mistake when asked 'How did you get your answer? This is possibly because their classroom experience has taught them that if an answer is not immediately accepted there must be something wrong with it. Generally, as the interview progresses pupils become less threatened by a request for their method; many come to expect to be asked this question and are happy to provide an account for the assessor.

The fact that some pupils do learn to regard questioning as part of their learning experience suggests that it is a matter of practice and convention. It also seems to be an approach worthy of cultivation, especially when it extends to pupils questioning their own and one another's approaches, as a matter of course.

In an interactive interview, or in a classroom setting, there are a number of ways that teachers can respond to pupils' queries. One is to be directive and give pupils the answers; another is to be non-directive and turn the query back to them and suggest that they take responsibility for deciding. This can be accomplished by saying 'It is up to you to decide', or 'You do what you think is right'. Another is to use probes or prompts which do not give them the answers, but perhaps help pupils use what they know or have worked out so far in their attempts to solve problems. All these possibilities are discussed in more detail below.

During their briefing sessions when assessors were trained to administer the tests, it was found that teachers who were not familiar with this type of approach took a while to get used to it. This has been found to hold true for many pupils as well. It requires both training and practice. Initially it can also be frustrating for pupils who are used to having answers provided. In the long run, though, it may encourage self-reliance and initiative as pupils learn to trust themselves and their judgements.

Phrasing of questions

The way questions are worded can markedly affect pupils' responses; often pupils have the requisite knowledge, but are thought not to because they do not answer the question asked. This is often because the question does not relate to their frames of reference and their ways of thinking about the problem. This means that there is sometimes a mismatch between the questions we ask and the questions pupils answer. An example of this was found in the Guess-a-Number topic, in which 11-year-olds are asked to make successive guesses at finding a target number, for example:

$$21 \times \boxed{} = 504$$

After each guess as to the value of ☐ , pupils are asked: 'What does that tell you about the number you are looking for?' (ie the target number).

A common response to a guess of $\boxed{27}$, say, is 'It's bigger' or to $\boxed{21}$ 'It's smaller'.

When questioned it emerges that pupils are referring to their current guess rather than to the target number. Eleven-year-olds seem to find it particularly difficult to verbalise the implications of their findings before they have discussed the facts.

A discussion was described earlier in which Jason, an 11-year-old, was asked to order the decimals 0.064, 0.35, 0.64, and 1.1 from smallest to biggest. In fact he started with the biggest number but questioning revealed that he was aware of this.

Describing and explaining

Pupils can be asked for a plan before the task is attempted, for an account while the activity is in progress or for *post hoc* descriptions and explanations. Asking for a plan before the task is attempted could be difficult for pupils and the resulting information is likely to be the least accurate. The oral descriptions of what pupils plan to do are often a poor reflection of what pupils actually do, when carrying out the task.

For example, pupils are asked to find the mass of one peg, given several pegs, a balance and a 20-gram mass. Before they use the apparatus they are asked to describe what they are going to do. Examples of responses to this question can be found in the first interviews on the APU videotapes for 11- and 15-year-olds. A typical response is:
> 'Put the 20-gram mass in one pan. Put enough pegs in the other until they balance. Count the pegs and divide.'

As can be seen, descriptions like these are of a very general nature and lack finer detail and precision. Is it that pupils do not see the need for more specific descriptions at this stage? Is it that they cannot articulate their plans precisely at this stage—for either developmental reasons, in the case of younger pupils, or lack of practice in the case of all pupils? Or is it that they make assumptions that the teacher will know what they mean, and therefore feel it unnecessary to go into detail?

The APU Mathematics Team's experience is similar to that of the APU Science Teams. In the Science surveys, when describing what they would do to find out which of a given number of wooden blocks would be most suitable as a chopping board, only about 5 per cent of pupils suggested or implied that they would subject each block to similar treatments. In practice, about 80 per cent of pupils *did* give the same kind of treatment to each block. This indicates a large discrepancy between what pupils said they would do and what actually happened.

Pupils who do not have a clear idea of how to carry out a task may lose confidence and make no attempt, rather than have a go. Of course, for some pupils it may have a different effect, namely that in trying to describe their strategies they may crystallise their ideas. This tends to be a less common occurrence.

Asking for an account while an activity is in progress might be done by the assessor saying 'As you are going along can you tell me what you are doing?' A problem with this is that verbalising while undertaking an activity could interfere with the smooth carrying out of the activity. Pupils working in groups, however, tend to discuss strategies as they are going along, and are able to modify ideas according to input and feedback from group members.

There may be instances where verbalising helps pupils to keep the task in focus. In one example an 11-year-old child was asked to find the area of this shape:

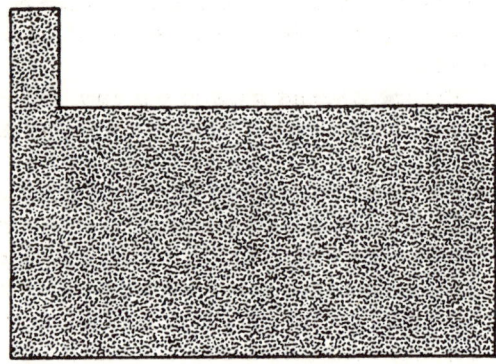

She had a grid and ruler available and chose the grid to count squares. She was then asked if she could check her answer using a transparent plastic ruler. She was unsure about this, but took the ruler and placed it along the top edge of the larger rectangle making up the shape. She counted up to 10, then moved her ruler down about 1 centimetre parallel to its initial direction, said '20', down again—'30'. Effectively, she was using the ruler as a grid, because she did not in fact know how to find the area by any other method. After reaching 30 she took the ruler off the paper and said, 'I've forgotten what I was doing.' She began the process again, spontaneously verbalising what she was doing, and was able to complete it.

Asking for *post hoc* explanations seems to be the easiest procedure as far as pupils are concerned and it sometimes has bonuses; often in providing *post hoc* explanations pupils discover errors they have made and self-correct them. For example, when telling assessors about a day out, many pupils realised that their plans did not quite match their intentions. They then modified their plans to take account of the task requirements.

However, some pupils feel that a change of plan is an admission of failure. In cases like this, rather than admit to an error, pupils will try to justify their incorrect or inadequate responses.

In summary, the pre-task descriptions were most general and least accurate and the post-task ones most detailed and accurate. The 'during-task' descriptions tended to be incomplete in many cases, as pupils often found it distracting to have to talk and 'do' at the same time.

Again, the experiences of the APU Science Teams have a bearing on the above findings; they suggest that planning an investigation is a much more linear activity than is performing one. In performance there are often unexpected snags which arise and which may be overcome or circumvented by changing strategy or restarting at an earlier part of the process. Plans generally do not anticipate problems and, indeed, can proceed on the basis of quite unrealistic approaches. Thus in plans there are normally well-defined steps to be identified, some of which depend on the previous steps, whilst others may be optional, in that their presence is not a prerequisite for the later steps (for example, results can be obtained without variables being controlled or equipment specified).

Being non-directive

We have mentioned that many of the practical assessors and other teachers who have been involved in APU work have said that one of the hardest things that has been required of them is to be non-directive and to avoid 'teaching'. However, without exception, having tried it, those teachers who had not consciously used the technique before said that they were pleasantly surprised (sometimes astounded) by the intellectual resources that the pupils tapped into when the initiative was left to them.

Being non-directive is not giving answers but encouraging pupils to seek them for themselves. For example, when a pupil asks, 'Should I do it like this, Miss?' the teacher says, 'Do it however you think best' or 'What do *you* think?' or 'That's up to you', rather than saying 'Yes' or 'No'.

In some situations it may be simpler or time-saving to give a direct answer or even petty not to. However, it seems likely that if pupils (and teachers) are to adapt to, and benefit from, this approach, it is necessary to encourage the habit of giving neutral responses.

There is a strong move towards pupils consulting one another about mathematics, as is emphasised in the Cockcroft Report[10]. It may be that pupil talk could be encouraged by suggesting that pupils consult one another, before they consult the teacher.

Prompting and probing

Often when pupils are asked questions or asked to carry out tasks there are points at which they seek clarification, more information or reinforcement. Similarly, when observing pupils at work or when talking to them, teachers need to assure themselves of how and why pupils are adopting particular strategies. At these times, the use of prompting or probing might be appropriate.

In our terminology a 'prompt' given by the assessor provides the pupil with some information to guide him or her towards a solution or a correct answer. By contrast, a 'probe' is a request by the assessor for information about what the pupil is doing or a clarification of what has been done. While it is not difficult theoretically to distinguish between a 'prompt' and a 'probe', in practice a probe, intended by the assessor to be a neutral request for clarification, may supply information. The classic case is saying after a pupil has given an answer, 'Are you sure?' Invariably this is interpreted by pupils as indicating that their answer was wrong. In an interactive situation pupils are very likely to interpret everything the assessor says or does as an indication of whether or not they are on the right track. A change in facial expression or an inflection in the voice are indicators. Nevertheless a question such as 'How did you get that?' has generally worked well as a neutral probe. It is used frequently when pupils work out answers mentally. Here is one example of an exchange relating to the question 'How many 17p stamps can you buy for £1?' The correct answer was given.

> Assessor: How did you get that?
> Pupil: I divided.
> Assessor: How did you divide?
> Pupil: Just divided. I said 17 into 100.
> Assessor: So how did you divide 17 into 100?
> Pupil: Well I know 3 17s is 51 because I play darts. Double it is 102 and so the answer's 5.

This exchange may appear more like an interrogation than a chat about mathematics. However this was due to the unfamiliarity of the question 'How did you get that?'; for the pupil did not initially know what was wanted. Once pupils are prepared for the question the discussion about methods becomes more relaxed and can produce some interesting ideas, as happened with this pupil.

A useful prompting technique is that of reviewing topics or information previously covered so that the pupil may suddenly 'see' an answer because he or she has included an important element hitherto neglected.

> Assessor: You started using the balance on one side; what were you going to do?
> Rachel: (hesitation then enlightened look)
> Oh—make both of them the same size. Should I do it?
> (Completes task successfully)

Prompting is used in several situations: when pupils are working in the right direction and are 'nearly there' but just need a nudge; when they are unable to make a start, possibly because they do not understand a term used; or, generally, when prompting is thought to be fruitful in providing information about a pupil's thinking. It is also a useful technique when pupils have got stuck, lost their way or have given a seemingly inadequate response.

In the 1979 practical survey it was permissible for assessors to provide prompts whenever they wished. There was considerable variation between assessors in the quantity and quality of the prompting. Thereafter general prompting was allowed only when scripted, although permission for the 'getting started' and 'nudges to finish' types of prompt was continued. Fruitful prompts which emerged from the 1979 survey and subsequent pilot work were incorporated into practical topic scripts with instructions to assessors about the conditions under when they could be used. Here are some examples:

i) *Encouraging the pupil to respond*
In the Guess-a-Number topic many pupils are very wary of making a guess, presumably because they are used to being asked for precise answers. So, if a pupil hesitates, there is a prompt: 'Just have a guess, you can have another go if it's wrong.'

ii) *Rephrasing the question*
If a question is not understood it can be rephrased using alternative or simplified wording. For example, initial questions may include technical terms, in order to judge pupils' reaction to them, but can be replaced with explanatory phrases if the pupils' knowledge of the term is not being assessed.

iii) *Focusing pupils' attention*
Some pupils may not know where to start a complex problem. For example, in one topic pupils are given the cost and weight of five different sizes of coffee tins and asked to work out which one is the best value for money. A calculator is available. Those who do not respond are asked to look first at the two smallest sizes and decide which of them is the better value.

iv) *Producing reflective thinking*
Some questions are tackled impulsively by pupils, whereas a little thought might enable them to use a more sophisticated method and so demonstrate a higher level of understanding. In a capacity/volume topic pupils are shown a wooden cube and a perspex box and asked to estimate how many cubes would fill the box. They are then presented with further cubes and asked to check their estimates with the proviso that they don't have to use all of the cubes. This is repeated for those pupils (17 per cent of 15-year-olds) who appear to be filling the box.

In a symmetry topic pupils are provided with two congruent rectangular sheets of paper. One is plain and the other has two diamond shapes drawn on it, placed symmetrically.

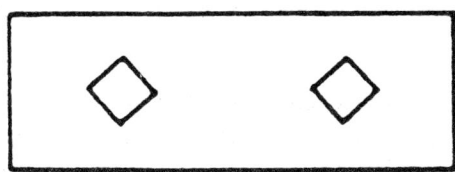

Pupils are asked to reproduce the pattern by folding and cutting the plain piece of paper. This can be done in a number of ways, the most direct being first to fold the paper in half parallel to a shorter side and then push the scissors into the paper to cut out the diamond shape. Other methods require more visualising of the situation. There are several methods using two folds and one using one lengthwise fold. Those who begin with the most direct method are halted when they attempt to push the scissors into the paper by being asked 'Can you think of a way of doing it without pushing your scissors into the paper?' If this produces no response, a further prompt is given; 'You can fold it more than once if you want.'

v) *Asking a simpler question*
Some questions require more than one step to produce a solution. Pupils unable to plan all the steps are prompted by being given a related question involving only one step. Thus, 15-year-olds unable to decide how to use a balance to produce a lump of plasticine one quarter as heavy as the piece they have before them are asked whether they could make one half as heavy.

Giving pupils time

Data from the attitude survey suggest that many pupils feel that teachers go too fast. Some pupils said:

> 'Maths should be taught at a slower pace than it is because this [how it is taught at present] does not give people enough time to understand it properly. And the teachers should be more understanding.'

> 'People like myself would do better if we had more time to understand the work we do and then we would be able to get better marks and also have a better knowledge of maths.'

In the practical survey interview, as in the classroom, it is often tempting to assume that if pupils do not supply immediate responses to questions they do not know the answers. However, this is not always the case; sometimes when pupils lack confidence they may hold back. In such situations, it may be necessary to draw the pupil out.

In the interview with Rachel (Age 11 video), she was asked to make a 10-gram lump of plasticine from a previously made 20-gram lump, using a balance. Initially she started to divide the plasticine, but then stopped and said, 'I don't get it' (what she is supposed to do) and 'Can't do it'. However, the assessor felt from her early movements that she did have some idea, so pursued the matter. After some prompting, she completed the task successfully.

It might have been tempting for the assessor to abandon this task when Rachel said she could not do it, but given that she had shown some non-verbal signs of an idea (she appeared to start dividing the plasticine) the assessor felt it was important for Rachel's confidence in her own performance to continue. It seems likely that many pupils, like Rachel, may never demonstrate their knowledge if their teachers do not recognise their reluctance and give them time to do so.

Recording

A feature of both the practical topics and written Problems and Patterns tests has been pupils' poor performance in recording findings or, in fact, seeing the need to do any recording. In the practical topic, Tiles, for example, which concerns number patterns related to maximum and minimum perimeters of different numbers of square tiles, pupils are willing to manipulate apparatus, but are reluctant to write down any notes or any numbers as to the various combinations and permutations they have tried. This means that when they are asked to evaluate their findings, they are unable to do so, because they have no written information on which to base further action, unless they have good memories.

More recently, in a group version of the same task, pupils have been asked to work together to find the biggest and smallest perimeters of different numbers of square tiles, given that the length of the side is one unit. In these situations the assessor has noted whether pupils record their results spontaneously or not. By and large, spontaneous recording is rare. Assessors, therefore, often have to encourage recording, and frequently have to remind pupils during the topic that this might be a useful technique.

It seems likely, too, that this lack of recording relates to a lack of practice as well as a lack of appreciation that recording of findings and results may form part of mathematical procedures.

When no structured record sheet is provided pupils often lose track of what they are doing because they have no written record of their previous findings. This was a problem for 11-year-olds in the Guess-a-Number topic; assessors had to give frequent reminders about recording. In that topic, though, some pupils were so keen to use their calculators that the recording of results was often viewed as an unwelcome interruption to pressing the keys.

Methods of recording

One problem pupils may have is knowing what and how to record. When they are asked to complete a structured record sheet in the form of a table with headed columns, they normally do so without difficulty. The types of recording the pupils use without the provision of a structured record sheet are worthy of note. Commonly, it does not seem that pupils give much thought to the best method of recording results. Most frequently, they will simply choose to list their findings without any attempt to systematise or cluster similar findings, possibly because they think that listing information is quicker than other methods. The task pupils are given might determine what is thought to be the most appropriate method of recording: bar charts may be appropriate for surveys, for example. The evidence from the written tests suggests that most pupils are able to construct bar charts when asked to do so. However, in practical work they are more likely to choose a form of recording which does not require much planning. For example, one pupil interviewed said she knew that she could have used a graph to represent the number of times each number on a die came up in 24 throws, but thought it would be quicker to make a single list of each outcome similar to IV in the diagram overleaf. Pupils using this method have first to sort out the written results before they can reach any conclusion or generalisation.

For example, 11-year-olds were asked to record the results of tossing a coin 12 times so that they could tell how often each outcome had occurred. Plain and squared paper were available; although the majority chose the latter, less than 10 per cent actually drew a block chart. Over a third of the pupils listed the outcomes in two separate columns. Here are four examples of recording on squared paper. Sometimes the actual results were as in (I), but more often tallies were made (II).

I	II	III	IV
head / tail head / tail head / tail head / tail head / tail / tail / tail	heads / tails 1 / 1 1 / 1 2 / 1 1 / 1 1 / 1 1 1	Head / tail 1 / 1 2 / 2 3 / 3 4 / 4 5 / 5 6 / 6	1 heads 2 tails 3 tails 4 tails 5 tails 6 tails 7 tails 8 heads 9 heads 10 tails 11 heads 12 heads

The effects of practice in recording were evident when working with pupils who were used to an investigative and project-based approach; recording was seen as an integral part of the activity and was generally superior. Examples of such pupils' work on the Tiles topic (investigating maximum and minimum perimeters of square tiles) are shown below:

Figure 1 Recording from group investigations of the Tiles topic (except where stated)

Age 11

No of Squares	Maximum	Minimum
3	8	12
4	10	16
5	12	20
7	16	28
2	6	8

Age 11

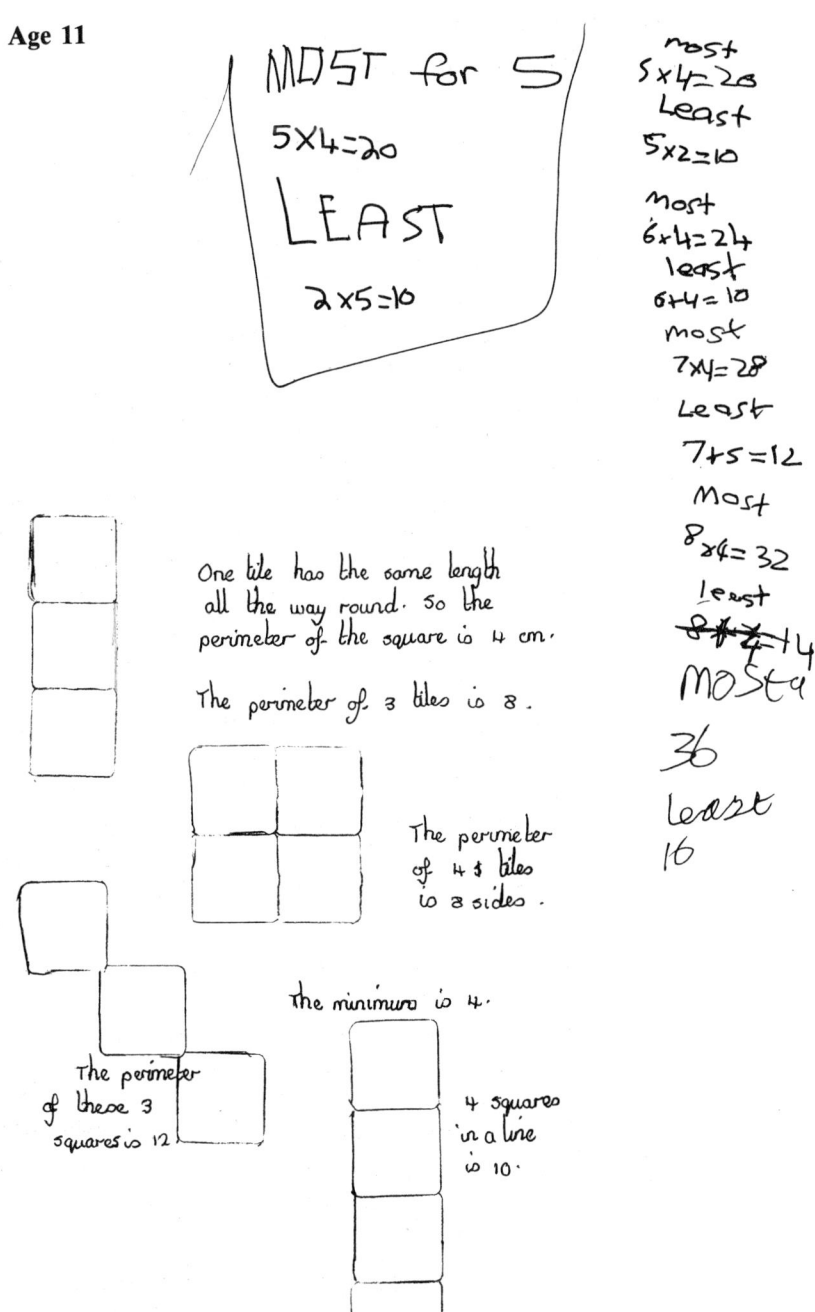

MOST for 5
5×4=20
LEAST
2×5=10

most
5×4=20
Least
5×2=10
most
6×4=24
least
6+4=10
most
7×4=28
Least
7+5=12
Most
8×4=32
least
8+4=14 (crossed out)
Most
36
Least
16

One tile has the same length all the way round. So the perimeter of the square is 4 cm.

The perimeter of 3 tiles is 8.

The perimeter of 4 tiles is 3 sides.

The perimeter of these 3 squares is 12

The minimum is 4.

4 squares in a line is 10.

continued overleaf

Figure 1 *(continued)*
Age 11 – *individual attempt*

My Investigation

(1) I have found that because each tiles edge is one unit the perimeter imediately becomes four units.

(2) Because each tile represents 4 units two seperate tiles represent 8 units so if you take two tiles and make them as one each tile now has three sides and so if you times the number of edges by the number of tiles you get the perimeter. If I had 4 tiles I would have two edges to each tile what would the perimeter be...?...

makes up question herself

(3) If I take 3 tiles and put them corner to corner then I have 4 sides to each tile then I would times the number of tiles by the number of sides I get the perimetre.

So overall you could say sides × tiles = perimeters

(4) ~~Because 4 tiles = 8 then 8 tiles would equal the amount of twice 4 tiles which = 8×2 = 16×~~

(4.) This rule only works with square numbers because the number of single sides made into two side is equal to the ones of twos sides already made making a square number.

(5) I have 45 tiles and because they do not make a square number my rule does not work with all of them.

(6) I tried doing my corner to corner rule and it worked ~~because the number of~~ ~~~~

(7) Some shapes, although its seems they can't, can work by my rule like for instance this one

Age 11

1) 4 units
2) 6 units min
   8 units max
3) 8 units min
   12 units max
4) 16 units max
   10 units min
5) 20 units max
   10 units min
6) 10 units min
   24 units max
7) 12 units min
   28 units max
8) 12 units min
   32 units max
9) 14 units min
   36 units max
10) 14 units min
    40 units max
11) 14 units min
    44 units max
12) 14 units min
    48 units max
13) 16 units min
    52 units max

15) 18 units min
    60 units max
20) 18 units min
    80 units max
16) 16 units min
    64 units max
17) 18 units min
    68 units max
18) 18 units min
    72 units max
21)

Kirsty age-11
St. Michael's School
11/7/85 Melksham

Age 15

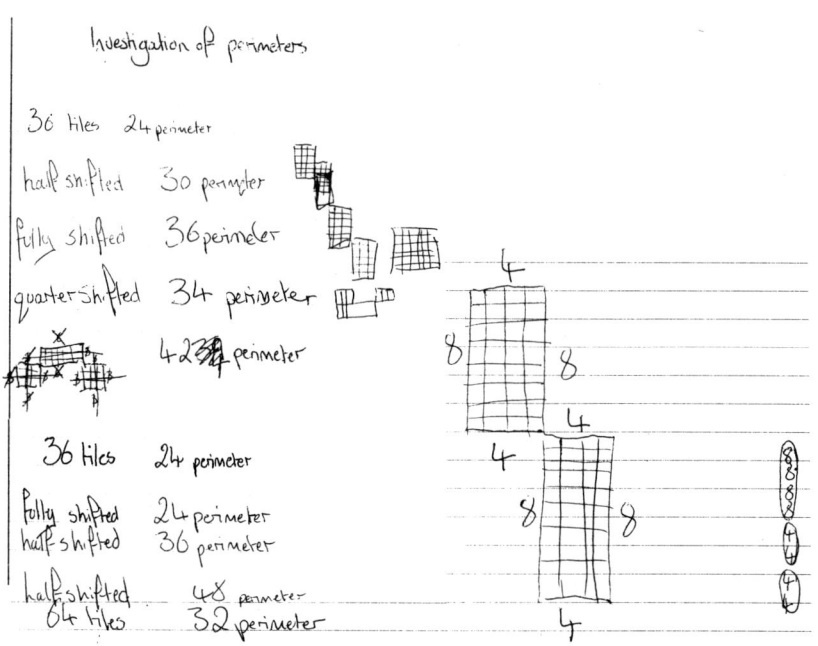

Investigation of perimeters

36 tiles   24 perimeter
half shifted   30 perimeter
fully shifted   36 perimeter
quarter shifted   34 perimeter
             42 34 perimeter

36 tiles   24 perimeter
fully shifted   24 perimeter
half shifted   36 perimeter

half shifted   48 perimeter
64 tiles   32 perimeter

continued overleaf

Figure 1 (continued)

Age 15

SQUARES 1 TILE SQUARE
1×1 PERIMETER = 4
2×2 square 4 TILE SQUARE PERIMETER = 8

x = sides
$x \times 4$ = Perimeter   3×3 square   9 TILE SQUARE PERIMETER 12

4×4 square   12 16 TILE SQUARE 16 PERIMETER 16

$x = \square$
∴ PERIMETER = $x \times 4$ 5×5 square   25 TILE SQUARE PERIMETER = 20

6×6 square   36 TILE SQURE PERIMETER 24

so if you find the length of x then multiply it by 4, you end up with the perimeter of the square.

10×10 SQUARE   100 TILE SQUARE PERIMETER = 40

ACCORDING TO THIS, A 20×20 SQUARE SHOULD HAVE A PERIMETER OF 80

let x = the number of tiles in a square. find the square root of x then multiply it by 4 to get the perimeter

No. of tiles in square → perimeter of square.
$x \rightarrow \sqrt{x} \times 4$
$x \rightarrow 4\sqrt{x}$

Comment

The time was sufficient and the tiles were ideal to solve the problem.

Age 15

Investigating perimetres.

1) [row of 4 squares]
2) [staircase of squares]

We decided to try to investigate to see if the two investigations above have the same perimetre.

We found that they hadn't because on investigation 1 2 sides were joined together so that it made one side but on investigation 2 only the corners were touching so therefore it had more sides and made the perimetre larger than that of investigation 2.

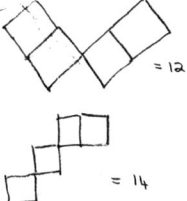
= 12
= 14

have the same number of squares but the way that they are laid out the perimetres are different.

number of Squares	number of edges		number of Squares	number of edges		number of Squares	number of perimetre
1	4		1	4		4	8
2	6		2	8		5	10
3	8		3	12		6	10
4	10		4	16		7	12
5	12		5	20		8	12
			6	24		9	14
						10	14

In Algebra 2x+2.

The table to show for this investigation.
[row of squares diagram]

In Algebra 4x.

The table is for this investigation
[staircase diagram]

There is no Algebra. We predict that 10 tiles would have the perimetre of 18. But it was 20.

The smallest perimetre of 4 squares. ●

The smallest perimetre is 10cm.

Pupils in this group commented, 'We needed more time and more tiles.'

continued overleaf

Figure 1 (continued)
Age 15

(Side = 1 unit.

2 ☐'s ⊞ = 8 sides every time (Joined Diagonally)
2 ☐'s ⊞ = 6 units " " (Joined Straight)
3 ☐'s ⊞ = 12 units every time (Joined Diagonally)
3 ☐'s ⊞ = 8 units not every time.

If you saw the tile diagonally every time the area never changes but the perimeter does (with the same no of squares (corners))

Age 15

1st pattern. Perimeter 32 units
2"   "   . "   24 "
3"   "   . "   12 "
4"   "   . "   20 "
5"   "   . "   26 "
6"   "   . "   14 "

There are other instances where pupils record efficiently and use the information thus gathered to make further reasoned decisions. In one example, the pupil, in trying to find a target number, said that the first guess was much too low and decided that doubling it would be appropriate. The next two guesses were much closer to the target.

Mathematical vocabulary

Thorndike (1913)[11] suggested that ability in arithmetic was a measure of two things—mathematical insight and acquaintance with language. There are many more research data to support the view that language development is likely to affect mathematics learning. The relationship is complex: it is not just a matter of decoding the actual words; what is needed is the comprehension of those words as they relate to mathematics and not to other areas of discourse. For example, it is not sufficient to be able to read or say 'difference', if the pupil then, in the context of a mathematics task like 'What is the difference between 1,000 and 99?', gives the answer that '1,000 is bigger' or '1,000 has four numbers but 99 has only two'.

Recently there has been growing interest amongst mathematics specialists about language and mathematics. Initially much of this work has focused on readability of mathematics texts and the effect of vocabulary on pupils' performance. The latter has been a feature of some APU items. In the written tests, the influence of mathematical terms can be seen clearly in the following items:

Example 1

Age 11

3 added to 14 makes . . .	What is the sum of 14 and 3?
97% answer correctly	82% answer correctly

Age 15

7458 + 5587	Find the sum of 7458 and 5587
94% correct	80% correct A further 5% attempt an addition, but compute incorrectly.

Age 11

Add 4.5 and 0.5	4.5 and 0.5 is . . .	What is the sum of 0.5 and 4.5?
68% correct	68% correct	58% correct

In subtraction, the following results emerge and, as can be seen, there are sometimes differences in response patterns when verbal descriptions and conventional notation are used.

Age 11

Take 36 away from 47	What is the difference between 47 and 36?	47 minus 36 makes . . .
92% correct	80% correct	65% correct

continued overleaf

Example 1 (continued)

Age 11

2.6 − 1.2 =	Take 1.2 away from 2.6	What is the difference between 2.6 and 1.2?	2.6 minus 1.2 makes . . .
80% correct	79% correct	61% correct	58% correct

Age 15

What is the cube of 4?	$4^3 = \ldots$
34% correct	57% correct

Similar results are also found for other types of items; for example, pupils were given a T-shaped figure with lengths of sides marked and asked to find the perimeter. The results for both age groups are as follows:

How far is it right round the edge of the shape?			What is the perimeter of the T-shape?		
	Age 11	Age 15		Age 11	Age 15
Correct	76%	84%	Correct	69%	70%

In looking into this issue, Earp and Tanner (1980)[12] found that 93 per cent of the 11-year olds in their study could decode (read and say) mathematical terms used frequently in mathematics schemes; however, they indicated understanding of only 50 per cent of them by explaining or using them appropriately in examples. Giving the term in a sentence from a textbook led to an 8 per cent increase in understanding.

Earp and Tanner contend that reading in mathematics is likely to be greatly improved when children speak the related language. In the classes they observed, mathematical language was not used extensively; seldom were there extensive periods in which mathematical terms were spoken. They found this particularly in classes where individualised schemes and numerous worksheets were used.

They suggest that mathematical vocabulary should be taught in similar ways to those used in reading classes with good introductions, rehearsal, language experience and structured review. The problem is that by the time pupils are 11, much of 'basic reading' teaching is assumed to be unnecessary.

> Oral emphasis in mathematics is recommended in that reading skills may thereby be increased. It has been noted that efforts given to improving reading in mathematics tend to be rewarded (Earp 1970). The additional process of making mathematical language a part of children's lives will further enhance these efforts.[13]

In mathematics, as in many other school subjects, key concepts are referred to by specialised terms, like 'parallel', 'factor', etc. However, as Otterburn and Nicholson (1976)[14] found, many pupils who are assumed to understand such terms do not. They found that pupils following a CSE syllabus in Northern Ireland did not fully understand commonly used mathematical terms, like 'product' and 'multiple' (Nicholson, 1977).[15]

Nicholson asked pupils to fill in missing words in sentences that they felt exemplified particular concepts, for example:

> 'The numbers 60, 90, 120 and 150 are all said to be ___ of 30.'

In the schools in which these studies took place the author reports that teachers felt that the tests revealed specific difficulties of which they had not been fully aware; they thought it a useful diagnostic exercise.

To give examples, some confused notions about parallelograms were:

> 'The sides are always straight and never meet.'
> 'They all have angles at the same degrees.'

Nicholson (1977) concluded from these studies that:

> 'these pupils who enter for CSE mathematics (broadly the middle 50% of the whole ability range) have significant difficulties in understanding some of the mathematical terms in common use. It is important that teachers should recognise the extent of their difficulties and work continuously for better understanding. To that end it is relatively simple to devise and administer short diagnostic tests'.[16]

As can be seen, APU survey results point to similar conclusions.

Summary and discussion points

This section has been concerned with mathematical literacy and oracy. The main discussion points made were:

i) *Oracy*
- Pupils' responses to questions are dependent on their perceptions of the meaning. The responses can be markedly affected by the phrasing of questions.
- The timing of questions in relation to a task (before, during or after) affect the accuracy of response, with the post-task being most detailed.
- Non-directive interaction provides opportunities for pupils to think for themselves. They need time to think.

ii) *Recording*
Unless provided with a structured table, pupils tend not to record their findings spontaneously. This is probably related to their lack of planning skills. Experience of seeing recording as an integral part of an activity improves performance.

iii) *Reading vocabulary*
Many pupils up to the age of 15 have difficulty with mathematical terms. It should therefore not be assumed that all pupils are fully conversant with the terms and the concepts they stand for once they have completed the topic in class.

4

Groups and group work

Introducing group work for the first time

Setting up group situations

Group work, although not new to most other school subjects, is not something that has been widely used in mathematics. Many teachers have expressed both interest and reservations about the appropriateness of group work in the mathematics classroom. However, most teachers who have braved the unknown have found the results rewarding and eye-opening.

When introducing group work for the first few times, especially to pupils who have no experience of it in mathematics, there are two important things to remember:

i) It may not work quite the way you anticipated, especially the first time; the teacher may not be sure what to expect and nor will the pupils.

ii) There are conventions governing group work that both teachers and pupils have to negotiate and come to grips with; for example, encouraging pupils to consult one another instead of the teacher, deciding what roles the individuals have in the group, how tasks are to be approached, what recording will be required, etc.

In class-based group work, there is a settling down period during which some pupils fool around. Others, though, merely seem to be experimenting with the novelty of the situation and, once they get used to it, seem to enjoy and profit from it.

What has surprised many teachers who have used APU topics is how little unfocussed talk goes on relative to that which is task-oriented. There is some playing about, but once pupils are involved they tend to concentrate well. However, there is evidence to suggest that the task pupils are asked to complete may be an important factor here; if pupils do not find the task interesting and involving, there may be much more off-task activity.[17]

When working with familiar ideas like a class trip, relatively little teacher input is required after the task has been set. Sometimes, though, it is necessary to inject some structure into the group situation if a particular outcome is a priority. Take record-keeping for example; in a topic about probability pupils were told, 'You must decide amongst yourselves how you are going to record your findings'. However, during the task they lost track because their record-keeping strategy had not been properly worked out before they started. It might have been a good idea for them to have established this before they began the task (with room for adaptation, of course, if it proved to be unworkable).

In APU-based group work, pupils have been told what the task is and have then been left, as far as possible, to work things out amongst themselves.

Some pupils find it difficult to know where to start. Often it helps if the teacher asks them what they think they are supposed to do. This invariably helps pupils clarify the problem for themselves and gives the teacher an idea of whether they have understood the task requirements.

If pupils do seem to have the general idea, the teacher could encourage them to begin by saying something like, 'Well, you seem to have the idea, now think of a way of using the apparatus/information you have on the table to find out what you need to know.'

How different pupils adapt to the group situation is interesting. One teachers' group reported that when planning a class trip, a group of four 11-year-olds decided that they would vote for particular options relating to meal times and activities. The same group also decided to take it in turns to do the necessary writing.

In another group, doing a similar task, teachers were impressed at how vigorously the pupils followed the task requirements—there was constant referral back to the requirements, more than was anticipated by the teachers.

Size and composition of groups

The appropriate size of a group may depend on the activity. For APU assessments, it was decided, after experimentation, that the optimal group size for most of our group work activities like planning a trip or classroom-based investigations was three pupils. Larger numbers tended to split into sub-groups and there were difficulties in some topics in sharing out the available resources. Two pupils working together were less interesting in terms of their social interaction than groups of three.

Early on in the development of APU group work, pupils were invited to choose their groups. However, this did not always work well. Friends were often operating at different levels in mathematics; and sometimes the highest-attaining pupils dominated the session so that pupils operating at a lower level lost track or were ignored—obviously something to be avoided.

In some cases, where mixed-attainment groups were used, the higher attainers were very conscious of the fact that there were lower attainers in the group. They seemed to be 'looking after' them; in the way that they spoke to them generally, by simplifying and explaining things, giving them tasks to do that they could manage, and accepting their contributions however irrelevant. On the strength of this experience, it was decided to group together pupils of similar attainment. This produced livelier and more balanced discussion which improved the quality of the group assessment.

Whether to mix boys and girls or not is a matter for consideration. In a classroom where group work may form a regular part of class organisation there may be opportunities for both.

In looking at this issue for assessment purposes, a few important issues arose; there were occasions in mixed groups of both ages where boys dominated and girls' contributions were not considered.

This observation is supported by much of the gender-related research (for example, Spender[18]), which suggests that girls are at a disadvantage in these types of settings. Group work of this type could, of course, be used as a forum to encourage girls and boys to examine how they react to one another in such situations—co-operatively and competitively—using the gender issue as a focus.

Another consideration which tends to point in favour of single-gender groupings is that of cultural norms. We have found that girls from particular ethnic backgrounds may be encouraged, as part of their upbringing, to accept what males say as correct; this may make it difficult for them to challenge the ideas put forward by boys in the group setting. They may put forward suggestions but often in a tentative way and may not feel confident about pressing their ideas home.

It is important to remember that these considerations about the groupings were governed by the need to facilitate a national monitoring survey. Your needs may be different, so your decisions about group size and composition may vary according to the setting in which group work takes place, the type of tasks set and the desired outcomes—for some situations larger groups, pairs of pupils, mixed-attainment groups or mixed-gender groups may be appropriate.

Advantages and difficulties of group work

The advantages are:

i) It gives pupils an opportunity to talk to other pupils about mathematics.

ii) Pupils often spark ideas off one another—a simple idea can often be elaborated into something more complex in which several pupils have a stake.

iii) Pupils have been known to do better at individual work when they also have experience of group work.

iv) Pupils often find it easier to see what other pupils have difficulty in understanding and can sometimes explain more clearly than can the teacher.

v) Pupils may find it easier to express their difficulties to people of their own age rather than the teacher. They may also be afraid to ask the teacher to explain yet again. They almost invariably say that they like working in a group, not just because of the social aspects, but because more ideas are contributed and evaluated.

vi) Pupils are often more motivated and involved than they normally are during mathematics lessons. Several teachers expressed surprise that pupils had spent two-and-a-half hours working on mathematics without realising it.

vii) Some teachers felt that pupils working on their own often keep to a very narrow channel, whereas in groups pupils can pool ideas.

Now for the difficulties encountered in the development of APU group work assessments. In many groups, it is quite easy to judge what contribution an individual has made. However, in others, particularly where one pupil is fairly silent, it is often difficult to gauge their levels of involvement and interest. Sometimes an individual who appears to be sitting back and saying nothing has opted out. In other groups, however, a pupil who has not said much for some time and who appears not to be participating suddenly comes out with the most pertinent comment of the session, often one that illustrates that everything that has been going on has been absorbed and assimilated.

Sometimes the assessor may not be able to follow what the participants are talking about. The APU findings are in line with those of Barnes and Todd (1977)[19] who suggest that the group members sometimes have an implied understanding amongst themselves to which outsiders (particularly adults) may not be privy. Barnes and Todd refer to the complex structures of tacit knowledge (of both social context and specific features of the task) that are used with great rapidity and fluidity during conversations within the group.

Another problem for an assessor is that group members often make references to 'it' or 'that' and it may be difficult for the outsider to decide what is being alluded to. As the conversation progresses it usually becomes more apparent what is being discussed. After the problem-solving session some of these points are clarified by talking to the pupils.

5
Assessment

Any part of APU work has assessment as a central issue. Assessments must be related to their purposes, which in the case of APU are to obtain a national picture of performance across a wide range of mathematics and to monitor changes in that picture over time. Such assessments as APU devises for its purposes are not necessarily immediately transferable to individual classrooms for diagnosing or evaluating the achievement of individual pupils.[20] However, there are assessment problems which are common to specific situations and the APU experience could have some light to throw on these problems. In this section we consider some issues which relate to assessing the broader range of mathematics which is encompassed by the national GCSE criteria for mathematics.

Assessment of descriptions and explanations

Oral and written descriptions and explanations by pupils are likely to be more prominent in the new GCSE curricula because of the requirements of the national criteria. Some categorising of this kind of response has been undertaken in APU practical and Problems and Patterns tests. One task pupils are given in the Mass topic is to find the mass of a small plastic tile using a balance, a 20-gram mass and a bag of tiles. They are first asked to describe how they will carry out the task. The typical responses given are differentiated and can be categorised or evaluated in several ways. For example:

Good answer. Precise details given, focuses on correct features of task.
> 'Put the mass in one pan and plastic tiles in the other until the pans are balanced, then count the number of tiles and divide 20 by that number to get the mass of 1 tile.'

Adequate answer. General outline given, focuses on correct features of task but final step not clear.
> 'Put the mass in one pan, add plastic tiles till the pans balance then divide.'

Inadequate answer. Partial focus on correct features of task, but does not give full details.
'Put the mass in one side and tiles in the other.'
'Put the mass in one side and one tile in the other.'

Such a scheme places pupils' responses on a dimension from inadequate to good and as such includes some negative features. It would be possible to view the responses in criterion-referenced terms, that is, as descriptions of what the pupils can do. The descriptions could be phrased positively and represent development in pupils' thinking about the use of a balance. Even the responses classed as 'inadequate' show some recognition of the way a balance is used. The adequate response recorded above represents a recognition of the use of a balance to measure the mass of a small object and a knowledge of the operation involved in calculating the mass.

The following example is taken from the written responses given to a written test item which was adapted by Foxman et al[21] from an APU Problems and Patterns test used at ages 11 and 15. The responses shown below were given by 14- and 15-year-old pupils.

Example 2

Jenny makes a set of patterns with shaded squares round lines of unshaded squares.

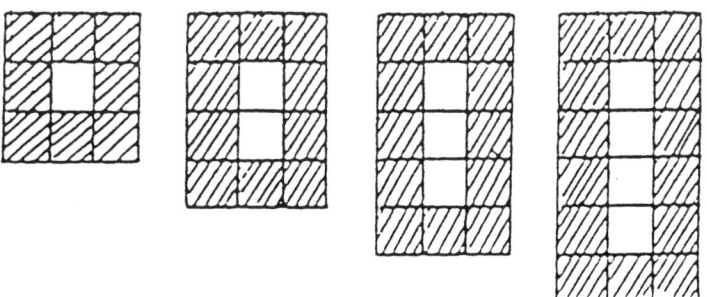

Pupils were first asked how many shaded squares would go round lines of 5, 8 and then 50 unshaded ones. They were then asked to write an explanation for the answer they gave to the latter question.

continued overleaf

Example 2 *(continued)*

I discovered a pattern between the numbers ie.
5 unshaded squares, 16 shaded
8   22 "
I then worked up to 75 unshaded squares using this method. My answer was 58 so I just doubled it and I got 116 shaded squares.

At first I drew a line of 50 squares and then realized it is much easier than I thought. I then added 50 + 50 and got 100 and then added 6, 3 from the top and 3 from the bottom to get 106.

I saw that if there were 50 unshaded squares, there will be 52 shaded squares on each side of the row.
Having doubled this figure to get both sides of the line of unshaded squares, I then added the two squares from the middle of both ends, making 106.

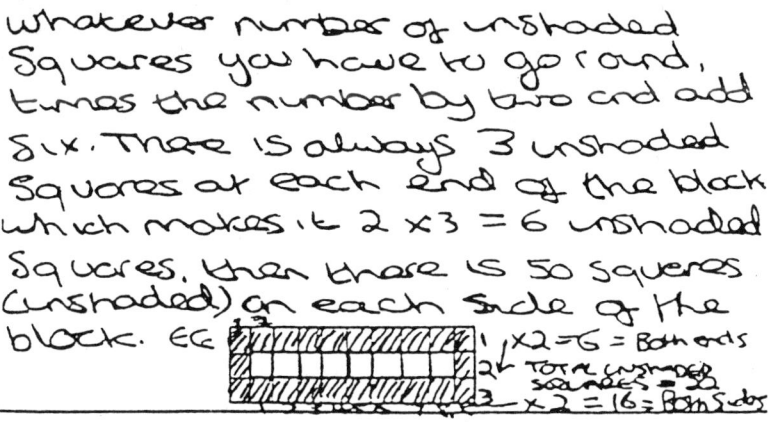

These four responses might be thought to differ in the precision of their language and the extent to which they are correct generalisations. In the first an arithmetical slip is made in calculating the number of shaded squares corresponding to 25 unshaded ones and an incorrect generalisation is then derived from it. The next two responses are clear descriptions of the process used, the second of this pair being given in more precise terms. The fourth response is a general rule. A slightly more sophisticated approach would be to use algebra.

These examples produce differentiated responses which could be used for diagnosing pupils' level of thinking. It should be emphasised, however, that until pupils are used to being asked to describe or explain in mathematics lessons, some of the less successful answers given to such questions could imply that these pupils do not appreciate what is being looked for.

Assessing groups and group work

The APU Mathematics Team, in their surveys of small-group problem-solving carried out in 1987, assessed a group outcome rather than the performance of individuals within the group.

At meetings with teachers to discuss group work, assessment has proved to be one of the most controversial aspects to arise. Some teachers contend that, if we are encouraging pupils to work together, we should accept one collaborative outcome—whether a written or an oral report or a design or construction of some sort. All members of the group would then get the same ratings. Other teachers are wary of this approach and would prefer pupils to submit individual pieces of work. They argue that if there are pupils who are not pulling their weight in the group it is not fair if they benefit from the work others put in. Perhaps the group members could be encouraged to regulate this. It is not always easy to decide quite how much each pupil has contributed to the work. There are cases where pupils appear to be on the periphery of the discussion, but on the rare occasions they do offer an idea it turns out to be a telling one.

Since the APU is not concerned with assessing individuals *per se* it seemed an obvious step to the team to assess the group as a whole, while noting the extent and type of interaction in which the group members engaged. The procedure which has been developed for the surveys divides each session into three phases.

In the first phase the assessor presents the problem, usually by setting a preliminary task in order to familiarise the pupils with the situation. During this phase the assessor interacts with the pupils, probing their understanding of the task and prompting where allowed. In the next phase, when the substantive problem has been given, the pupils are on their own; the assessor simply records the group processes. Finally, in phase three, when the group decide they have resolved the problem or gone as far with it as they can, they report their findings to the assessor, who clarifies what they did and why they did it. There are several facets to the assessment which will be described in more detail in the reports of the surveys. For the present booklet we consider some of the general ratings of the group performance. These included ratings of the following:

i) *Social interaction*
There are two ratings; one of them is the extent of the co-operation between group members. The other is concerned with the type of group (eg was it dominated by one authoritarian member, or led by a 'chairperson', or was it leaderless, but with everyone equally involved?).

ii) *Awareness of problem*
This category is concerned with the group's overall approach or strategy, which may be revealed at any stage of their working on the substantive problem.

iii) *Working on the task*
This is related more to the way in which the pupils work on the problem in accordance with their idea of what the problem is; that is,

the tactics they use in attempting to solve the problem. It concerns the concepts, skills and processes used during their work.

iv) *Communication*
Both within group and between group and assessor, communication is rated. It takes into account the oral, written, graphic, symbolic and other means they use in relation to the context of the communication and the way in which members of the group put forward ideas.

v) *Attitudes*
These ratings refer to pupils' involvement, persistence and enjoyment of the task. The ratings are derived partly from the assessor's observation and partly from the post-session interview.

The rating scales have four points, each of which has a general description. It has emerged, however, that these general descriptions need to be interpreted for performance on specific topics and that not all the scales are relevant to specific topics. Thus, in addition to the general ratings, assessors were given a schedule of ratings for each individual topic.

As already indicated, some further details of these assessments and, of course, the results from the small-group surveys of 11- and 15-year-olds in 1987 will be published in a separate report.

* * *

This booklet has been mainly concerned with some issues raised by the idea of discussion between pupil and teacher and among pupils themselves. These are two of the six opportunities pupils need to be provided with which were listed in paragraph 243 of the Cockcroft Report[10]. The Committee thought that these two opportunities were largely missing in schools. Their importance has been highlighted in the GCSE national criteria for mathematics. While the idea of practical mathematics is becoming reasonably clear, what constitutes mathematical oracy has not yet emerged in focus. It is of interest that most, if not all, the purposes of oracy outlined by the APU Language team would be applicable to mathematical situations. These are:

Describing and specifying
Informing/expounding
Instructing/directing
Reporting
Narrating
Arguing/persuading

Focused questions
Collaborative discussion/
   evaluation of evidence
Speculating/
   advancing hypotheses

In this booklet issues that the APU Mathematics Team feel are important have been highlighted: you may well have other observations to make. We would like to hear your views and would welcome correspondence to:

Derek Foxman
Head of the Curriculum Studies Department
National Foundation for Educational Research
The Mere
Upton Park
Slough SL1 2DQ

Notes

1. We are particularly indebted to Dr Margaret Maclure, formerly of the APU Language Team, now at the University of East Anglia, Department of Education, for her suggestions relating to this section of the study.

2. FOXMAN D D (1987). *Practical Mathematics—Assessing Practical Mathematics in Secondary Schools*. Windsor: NFER-Nelson (for Department of Education & Science, Assessment of Performance Unit).

3. FOXMAN D D, RUDDOCK G J and THORPE J S (1989). *Graduated Tests in Mathematics*. Windsor: NFER-Nelson (for Department of Education & Science).

4. FOXMAN D D (1987), op. cit.

5. GORMAN T P, et al (1984). *Language Performance in Schools: 1982 Primary Survey Report*. London: Department of Education & Science, Assessment of Performance Unit.

6. FLANDERS N H (1970), quoted in GORMAN T P et al (1984), ibid.

7. SHUARD H (1985). Presentation given at South Bank Polytechnic, London.

8. SPENDER D (1981). *Invisible Women*. London: Writers and Readers Publishing Co-operative.

9. Other interpretations of pupils' difficulties with ordering decimals can be found in MASON K P and RUDDOCK G J (1986). *Decimals: Assessment at Age 11 and 15*. Windsor: NFER-Nelson (for Department of Education & Science, Assessment of Performance Unit).

10. *Mathematics Counts* (1982). Report of the Committee of Inquiry into the Teaching of Mathematics in Schools. (Chairman: Dr W H Cockcroft). London: HMSO. The six opportunities alluded to on p53 are: 'exposition by the teacher; discussion between teacher and pupils and between pupils themselves; appropriate practical work; consolidation and practice of

fundamental skills and routines; problem solving, including the application of mathematics to everyday situations; investigational work.'

11   THORNDIKE E L (1913). *The original nature of man*. Columbia: University Press.

12   EARP W N and TANNER F W (1980). 'Mathematics and language'. *Arithmetic Teacher*, 28, 4. pp. 32–34.

13   Earp W N and Tanner F W, op. cit.

14   OTTERBURN M K and NICHOLSON A R (1976). 'The Language of [CSE] Mathematics', *Mathematics in School*, 5, 5.

15   NICHOLSON A R (1977). 'Mathematics and language'. *Mathematics in School*, 6, 5.

16   NICHOLSON A R, op. cit.

17   PIRIE S (1986). Presentation given at meeting of British Society for Research into Learning Mathematics, 20 September.

18   SPENDER D (1981), op. cit.

19   BARNES D and TODD F (1977). *Communication and Learning in Small Groups*. London: Routledge and Kegan Paul.

20   An NFER Review of assessments for low attainers (Graduated Test Project) found several CSE mode 3 examinations had incorporated APU-style one-to-one practical tests.

21   FOXMAN D D, RUDDOCK G J and THORPE J S, op. cit.

Acknowledgements

The APU Mathematics Team would like to thank all the teachers, LEA advisers and inspectors and pupils who have helped in the development work for this booklet, particularly those in the Surrey, Wiltshire and Somerset LEAs. The Surrey Media Resources Unit filmed many sequences; we acknowledge their contribution and thank them.